Elves, Fairies, & Gnomes

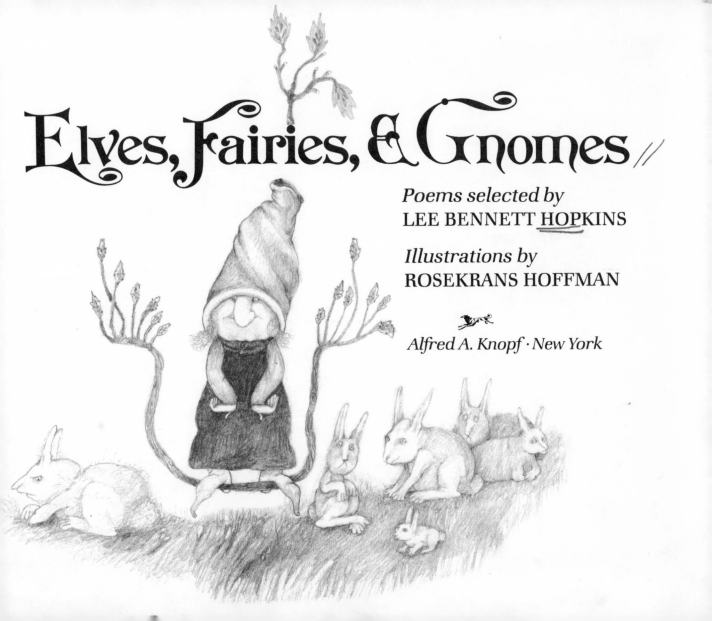

Elves, Fairies, & Gnomes

Poems selected by
LEE BENNETT HOPKINS

Illustrations by
ROSEKRANS HOFFMAN

Alfred A. Knopf · New York

For Barbara M. Hales—
Appropriately
Affectionately
and
Merry—derry—ly!

L.B.H.

In honor of
Helen Wohlberg and
Frances Means

R.H.

This is a Borzoi Book published by Alfred A. Knopf, Inc.

Text Copyright © 1980 by Lee Bennett Hopkins. Illustrations Copyright © 1980 by Rosekrans Hoffman. All rights reserved under International and Pan-American Copyright Conventions. Published in the United States by Alfred A. Knopf, Inc., New York, and simultaneously in Canada by Random House of Canada Limited, Toronto. Distributed by Random House, Inc., New York. Library of Congress Cataloging in Publication Data Main entry under title: Elves, Fairies & Gnomes. Summary: A collection of 17 poems about elves, fairies, and gnomes. 1. Fairy poetry. 2. Children's poetry. [1. Fairies — Poetry. 2. American poetry—Collections. 3. English poetry—Collections] I. Hopkins, Lee Bennett. II. Hoffman, Rosekrans. PN6110.F315 821′.008′0375 79-19753 ISBN0-394-84351-7 ISBN 0-394-94351-1 lib. bdg. Manufactured in the United States of America. Book design by Mina Greenstein. 10 9 8 7 6 5 4 3 2 1

Acknowledgments

Every effort has been made to trace the ownership of all copyrighted material and to secure the necessary permissions to reprint these selections. In the event of any question arising as to the use of any material, the editor and the publisher, while expressing regret for any inadvertent error, will be happy to make the necessary correction in future printings.

Grateful acknowledgment is made to the following for permission to reprint the copyrighted material:

Curtis Brown, Ltd.: "The Dance Has Ended" by Lee Bennett Hopkins. Copyright © 1980 by Lee Bennett Hopkins.

Doubleday & Company, Inc.: "The Elf Tree", copyright 1926 by Doubleday & Company, Inc., from TAXIS AND TOAD STOOLS by Rachel Field. Reprinted by permission of the publisher.

Elsevier-Dutton Publishing Co., Inc.: "Midsummer Magic" by Ivy O. Eastwick from FAIRIES AND SUCHLIKE. Copyright 1946, by E. P. Dutton & Co., Inc., copyright renewed 1974 by Ivy O. Eastwick. Reprinted by permission of the publisher, E. P. Dutton.

Barbara M. Hales: "Do Fairies Like the Rain?" by Barbara M. Hales. Used by permission of the author who controls all rights.

Harper & Row, Publishers, Inc.: "The Plumpuppets" from THE ROCKING HORSE by Christopher Morley (Lippincott). Copyright 1919, renewed 1947 by Christopher Morley. Reprinted by permission of Harper & Row, Publishers, Inc.

Contents

Elves, Fairies, & Gnomes

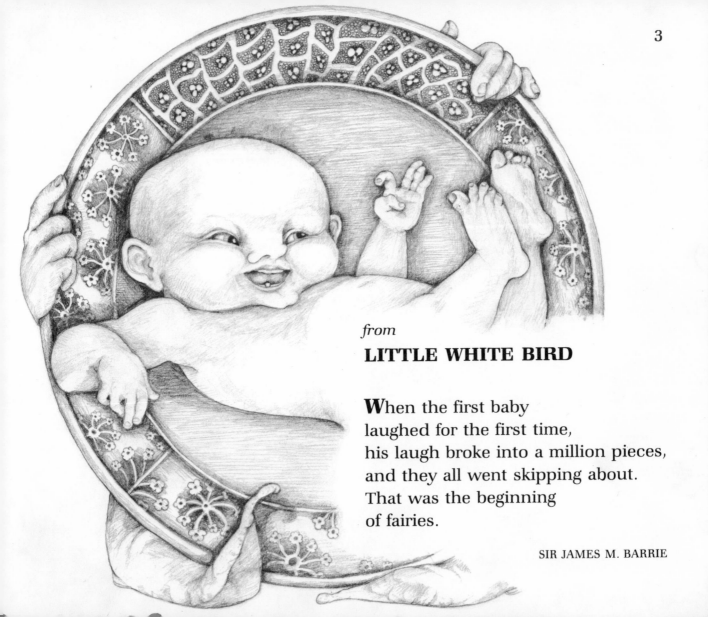

from

LITTLE WHITE BIRD

When the first baby
laughed for the first time,
his laugh broke into a million pieces,
and they all went skipping about.
That was the beginning
of fairies.

SIR JAMES M. BARRIE

I KEEP THREE WISHES READY

I keep three wishes ready,
Lest I should chance to meet,
Any day a fairy
Coming down the street.

I'd hate to have to stammer,
Or have to think them out,
For it's very hard to think things up
When a fairy is about.

And I'd hate to lose my wishes,
For fairies fly away,
And perhaps I'd never have a chance
On any other day.

So I keep three wishes ready,
Lest I should chance to meet,
Any day a fairy
Coming down the street.

ANNETTE WYNNE

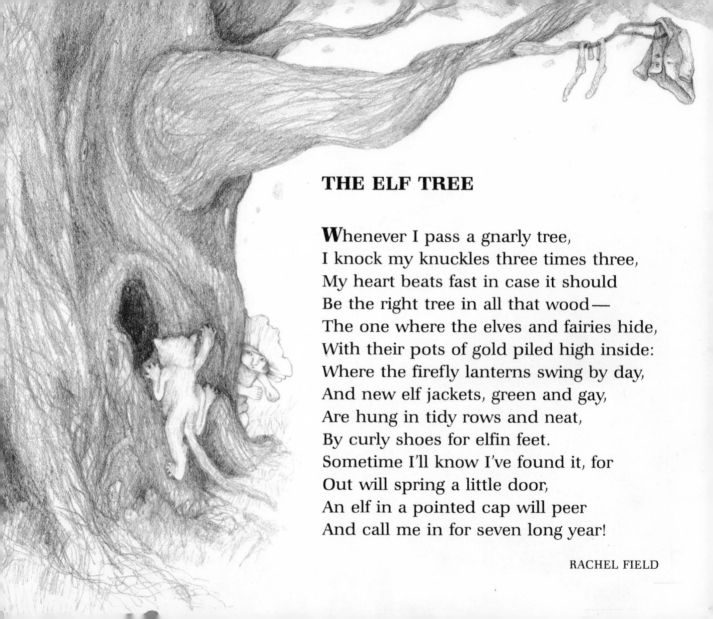

THE ELF TREE

Whenever I pass a gnarly tree,
I knock my knuckles three times three,
My heart beats fast in case it should
Be the right tree in all that wood—
The one where the elves and fairies hide,
With their pots of gold piled high inside:
Where the firefly lanterns swing by day,
And new elf jackets, green and gay,
Are hung in tidy rows and neat,
By curly shoes for elfin feet.
Sometime I'll know I've found it, for
Out will spring a little door,
An elf in a pointed cap will peer
And call me in for seven long year!

RACHEL FIELD

THE SEVEN AGES OF ELF-HOOD

When an Elf is as old as a year and a minute
He can wear a cap with a feather in it.

By the time that he is two times two
He has a buckle for either shoe.

At twenty he is fine as a fiddle,
With a little brown belt to go round his middle.

When he's lived for fifty years or so
His coat may have buttons all in a row.

If past threescore and ten he's grown
Two pockets he has for his very own.

At eighty-two or three years old
They bulge and jingle with bits of gold.

But when he's a hundred and a day
He gets a little pipe to play!

RACHEL FIELD

FAIRY FOLKS

Fairy folks
Are in old oaks!

ANONYMOUS

FAIRY VOYAGE

If I were just a fairy small,
I'd take a leaf and sail away,
I'd sit astride the stem and guide
It straight to Fairyland—and stay.

ANONYMOUS

THE FAIRY HOUSE

I've found a fairy house at last—I found it yesterday.
I found it in a little wood where I had gone to play.
I found it by a winding path which led me to the door,
And none, I'm sure, but fairy folk had traveled it before.

Outside it's just exactly like a very old oak tree,
But, oh, the door was open, and I couldn't help but see
The little mushroom tables and the little toadstool chairs,
And such a funny little step that led away upstairs.

A mossy rug was on the floor, so very smooth and neat.
I looked and looked and thought I saw the print of fairy feet.
A hammock made of spider lace was swinging to and fro,
To rock the fairy babies in at sleepy time, you know.

I hadn't been invited, so of course I couldn't stay.
Besides the little fairy folk all chanced to be away.
And so I kissed a clover leaf and hung it on the wall,
To tell the fairy family that I had been to call.

MAY JUSTUS

from

QUEEN MAB

A little fairy comes at night,
Her eyes are blue, her hair is brown,
With silver spots upon her wings,
And from the moon she flutters down.

THOMAS HOOD

from

THE FAIRY QUEEN

Come, follow, follow me,
You, fairy elves that be:
Which circle on the green,
Come follow Mab your queen.
Hand in hand let's dance around,
For this place is fairy ground.

ANONYMOUS

MIDSUMMER MAGIC

Midsummer Eve, a year ago, my mother she commanded,
"Now don't you go a'running down to Ragwort Meadow!
And don't you go a'plucking of the bracken seed or nightshade;
Stay out of the moonlight, mind! and keep out of the shadow,
For they say that the Ragtag,
                Bobtail,
                Merry-derry
                Fairy-men
Tonight will go a'dancing down in Ragwort Meadow."

Midsummer Eve, a year ago, my mother she commanded,
"Now don't you go a'playing down in Ragwort Meadow!
Keep away from thorn-tree, from adder's tongue and henbane!
Keep away from moonlight and don't venture in the shadow,
For they say that the Ragtag,
                Bobtail,
                Merry-derry
                Fairy-men
Are out a'snaring mortals down in Ragwort Meadow."

I wouldn't heed my mother's words! I wouldn't heed her warning!
I ran through the moonlight, through the starlight and the shadow!
And I never stopped a'running though my breath came quick and grasping,
Till I reached the very middle of Ragwort Meadow,
And there I heard the Ragtag,
> Bobtail,
> Merry-derry
> Fairy-men
A'laughing fit to kill themselves in Ragwort Meadow.

I heard 'em! But I couldn't see, no! not a little sight of 'em!
I pulled a curly bracken-leaf a'growing in the meadow,
I scratched out all the bracken-seeds and rubbed them on my eyelids—
The moon gave brilliant sunlight! There wasn't any shadow!
And there I saw the Ragtag,
             Bobtail,
             Merry-derry
             Fairy-men
A'dancing round me in a ring in Ragwort Meadow.

Half-a-hundred fairy-men and half-a-score of rabbits;
Half-a-dozen squirrels down in Ragwort Meadow,
Dancing round me in a ring—you never saw the like of it!—
Underneath the daylight which the bright moon shed! Oh!
A blessing on the Ragtag,
             Bobtail,
             Merry-derry
             Fairy-men
Who showed themselves to me down in Ragwort Meadow.

IVY O. EASTWICK

DO FAIRIES LIKE THE RAIN?

Do Fairies like a rainy day?
No! They hide and cry;
Their filmy wings — if they got wet
Would sag, and never fly.

Rain drops, rain drops,
Leave the Fairies be!
Fall upon the Leprechaun
Or Mermaids in the sea.

Do Pixies like a rainy day
A-piping through the dell?
The Pixies must enjoy the rain;
That's when they weave their spell.

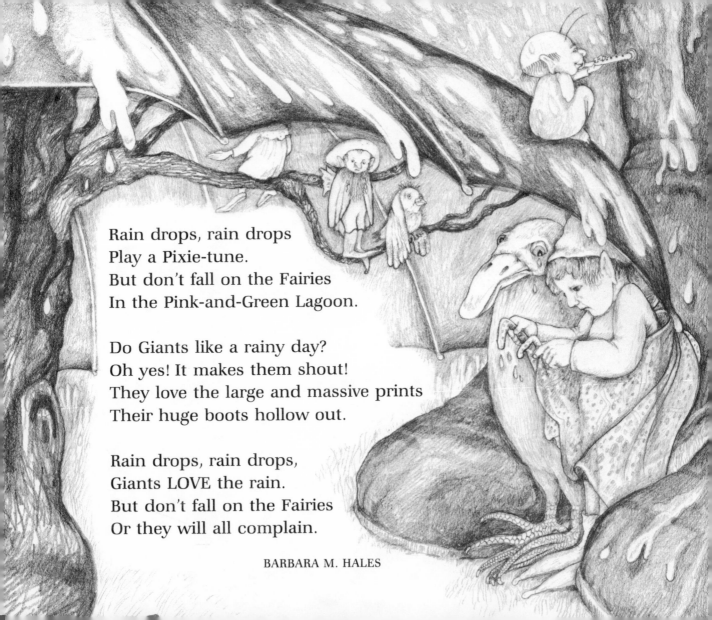

Rain drops, rain drops
Play a Pixie-tune.
But don't fall on the Fairies
In the Pink-and-Green Lagoon.

Do Giants like a rainy day?
Oh yes! It makes them shout!
They love the large and massive prints
Their huge boots hollow out.

Rain drops, rain drops,
Giants LOVE the rain.
But don't fall on the Fairies
Or they will all complain.

BARBARA M. HALES

THE DANCE HAS ENDED

Thirteen raindrops fell
signaling the beginning
of the dance's end.

LEE BENNETT HOPKINS

NO FAIRIES

"No fairies," said my mother
"There are no fairies, dear!"
But, oh, I wish my mother
Would stop with me to hear
The lily bells in evening chime,
And see the dew drops gleam,
And notice how the mosses bend
With green weight near a stream.

I wish she'd watch the grasses dance
And see the flowers nod,
And look at places tiny feet
Have worn away in sod,
And then, though she'd not see them,
I think she'd change her mind.
It doesn't mean "no fairies"
Because they're hard to find.

SOLVEIG PAULSON RUSSELL

THE PLUMPUPPETS

When little heads weary have gone to their bed,
When all the good nights and the prayers have been said,
Of all the good fairies that send bairns to rest
The little Plumpuppets are those I love best.

If your pillow is lumpy, or hot, thin and flat,
The little Plumpuppets know just what they're at;
They plump up the pillow, all soft, cool and fat—
    The little Plumpuppets plump-up it!

The little Plumpuppets are fairies of beds:
They have nothing to do but to watch sleepy heads;
They turn down the sheets and they tuck you in tight,
And they dance on your pillow to wish you good night!

No matter what troubles have bothered the day,
Though your doll broke her arm or the pup ran away;
Though your handies are black with the ink that was spilt—
Plumpuppets are waiting in blankets and quilt.

If your pillow is lumpy, or hot, thin and flat,
The little Plumpuppets know just what they're at;
They plump up the pillow, all soft, cool and fat—
The little Plumpuppets plump-up it!

CHRISTOPHER MORLEY

from

THE FAIRIES OF THE CALDON LOW

Then take me on your knee, mother;
And listen, mother of mine.
A hundred fairies danced last night,
And the harpers they were nine.

MARY HOWITT

FAIRIES

I cannot see fairies,
I dream them.
There is no fairy can hide from me;
I keep on dreaming till I find him:
There you are, Primrose! —I see you,
Black Wing!

HILDA CONKLING

from

PETER PAN

Whenever a child says,
"I don't believe in fairies,"
there's a little fairy somewhere
that falls right down dead.

SIR JAMES M. BARRIE

Lee Bennett Hopkins and Rosekrans Hoffman first collaborated on Go to Bed! A Book of Bedtime Poems, *a companion volume to* Elves, Fairies & Gnomes.

Lee Bennett Hopkins

is the editor of numerous popular poetry anthologies, and has written a variety of professional texts and articles. His novels for young people include *Mama* and *Wonder Wheels* (both Knopf).

He lives in Scarborough, New York.

Rosekrans Hoffman

received her B.F.A. from the University of Nebraska and worked in a variety of art-related jobs before turning to children's books full-time. Her growing list of distinctive picturebooks includes *Alexandra the Rock-Eater* and *My Mother Sends Her Wisdom.*

She lives in West Haven, Connecticut.